Date _____

This book belongs to

_____

Presented by

_____

Little Acts of Grace 2

Rosemarie Gortler and Donna Piscitelli

Illustrated by Mimi Sternhagen

Our Sunday Visitor Publishing Division
Our Sunday Visitor, Inc.
Huntington, Indiana 46750

Nihil Obstat: Rev. Paul F. deLadurantaye
Censor Librorum

Imprimatur: ✠ Paul S. Loverde
Bishop of Arlington
July 30, 2010

Except where otherwise noted, Scripture citations used in this work are taken from the *Catholic Edition of the Revised Standard Version of the Bible* (RSV), copyright © 1965 and 1966 by the Division of Christian Education of the National Council of the Churches of Christ in the United States of America. Used by permission. All rights reserved.

Some Scripture excerpts are taken from the *New American Bible with Revised New Testament and Psalms*, copyright © 1991, 1986, 1970, Confraternity of Christian Doctrine, Inc., Washington, D.C. Used with permission. All rights reserved. No part of the *New American Bible* may be reproduced by any means without permission in writing from the copyright owner.

Our Sunday Visitor Publishing Division
Our Sunday Visitor, Inc.
200 Noll Plaza
Huntington, IN 46750
1-800-348-2440
bookpermissions@osv.com

ISBN: 978-1-59276-795-3 (Inventory No. T1100)
LCCN: 2010931393
Cover and interior design by Amanda Falk
Cover and interior art by Mimi Sternhagen

PRINTED IN THE UNITED STATES OF AMERICA

Dear Children,

Do you know who loves you and forgives you and cares for you, no matter what you do or say?

Mom and Dad? Grandma and Grandpa?

That's right. But there is someone who loves you even more than they do, more than there are stars in the sky and more than all the grains of sand at all the beaches of the world! And He loves Mom, Dad, Grandma, Grandpa, and everyone else that way, too.

It's hard to imagine that much love, isn't it?

That's the way Jesus loves us! Think about it. God — who is much more important than a king, or a president, or even the pope — sent His Son to us as Jesus, a tiny baby, born in a stable with a crib lined with hay. Jesus is our Lord, our King and our Savior, but He said He wants to be our Best Friend, too. Living life with Jesus as our Best Friend brings a happier life and the peace in our hearts that only the love of Jesus can bring.

Share His friendship. Adore Him as God, but be a friend to Him, too. He will love that!

God bless you.

Rosemarie and Donna

Introduction

Guess who is your very best friend?
      Give up?
It's JESUS!
Jesus told us He is our Friend.
      He said, "I call you friends."
He's our God, but our very Best Friend, too.
He's everyone's Best Friend!

You can't imagine how MUCH He loves us!
      He wants to know all about us.
And He loves doing wonderful things for us,
      big things
         and little things.

Best friends do things for each other
      and know all about each other.
Jesus is such a good Friend,
      so it's important to get to know Him,
        and to do things for Him, too!

Doing little things for our friends
helps us know them better.
Jesus told us that when we do
kind things for others,
we are doing these things for HIM, too.

We can do little things in prayer,
in church,
at Mass,
and in so many other ways.

These little things we do
are loving acts of grace
that please our Best Friend
and keep us close to Him.

*"I have called you friends, because I have told you
everything I have heard from my Father."*
(John 15:15 – NAB)

Seeing the Lord in the Little Things

Our Best Friend, Jesus, loves it
    when we look for Him
        in the little things around us.

Like the times we notice
    the beauty God gave us
like noticing the statues in a church,
    and getting to know what the statues are all
    about.
And noticing the beauty
    of the stained glass windows.
When the sun is streaming through,
    the stained glass windows look like precious
    jewels!

Sometimes, these windows are pictures of people —
    Jesus, Mary, Joseph, and other saints.
Sometimes they show pictures
of things that happened —
    like Jesus walking on water.

Taking the time to notice the pictures and statues
and to think or read about the lives of the
saints
is a little act of grace
that helps us know and feel close to Jesus
through Mary and the saints.
Mary and the saints are all best friends with Jesus.

We keep pictures in our home and in
scrapbooks.
We hang them on our walls,
and we like to look at them.
These pictures help us feel close to
the people we love.

The statues and the stained glass windows in church
help us to think about the life of Jesus
and help us feel close to our Savior
and Best Friend, Jesus!

*On the walls round about in the inner room and the
nave were carved likenesses of cherubim.*
(Ezekiel 41:17–18)

Friends Like to Visit Each Other

Did you know that
      every single Sunday
            is a celebration of Easter Sunday?

Easter Sunday was the day
      Jesus rose from the dead!
Our faith tells us we *have* to go to Mass every Sunday
      to recognize this wonderful celebration.
But you know what?

Jesus, our Best Friend,
      is waiting for us there
         and appreciates when
           we **choose** to visit Him
even if we really feel like sleeping in
      or watching TV.
Jesus is really and truly there
waiting for **us** — His good friends — to visit!

When we **choose** to go to Mass,
we are going to a special meeting
      with our Friend.

The church is Jesus' house!

And He is right there in the church,
    waiting for us!

We know we can talk to Jesus anywhere.
But — at Mass,
    our prayers are especially heard.

This is why **choosing** to visit Jesus at Mass
rather than going because we *have* to
    is such a wonderful act of grace,
and shows how much we love Jesus.

*"Therefore you must keep the Sabbath as something
sacred."* (Exodus 31:14 – NAB)

Joining the Celebration

Mass is meant to be a joyful hour —
    especially when we think about
        what is really happening at Mass!
The love of our Best Friend,
    Jesus,
        is being remembered.
But being joyful is not the same thing as
being playful.

When we fold our hands to pray,
    our fingers point upward to God.
    That shows Him we are thinking of Him.

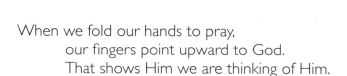

When we sit,
    or kneel,
        or stand with everyone else,
we are choosing to join in the celebration
    of the Mass
with all of Jesus' friends.
    That is really special!

St. Augustine said,
    "Singing is praying twice."
It is beautiful act of grace to join in with the hymn
    that is being sung,
        or the prayer
           that the priest is leading.
And you know what?
With so many voices singing and praying together,
    we become one voice,
        offering one song
           one prayer to Christ,
               our Lord and Friend.

And you know what else?
This same Mass is being celebrated all over the world!
It's like being at a party
    where the **whole world** is celebrating
        Jesus, our Savior and Friend, as the
Guest of Honor.

"For where two or three are gathered in my name, there am I in the midst of them." (Matthew 18:20)

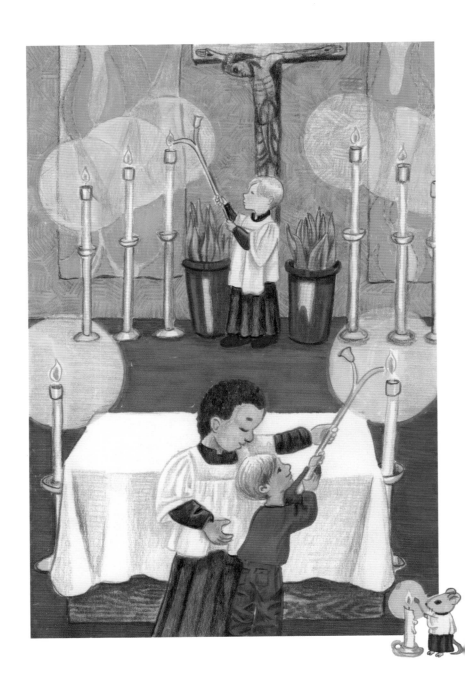

Jesus, the Light of the World

Notice the candles on or around the altar.
You've seen the altar server come out
    and light the candles before Mass.

Why do they do that?

It's not because it's too dark in church!

Jesus told us, "*I am the light of the world.*"
So the candles remind us of His special light.
The candles are also a way to show
    the joy
    and celebration
    of the Mass.

Lighting candles before Mass glorifies God!
    What an act of grace!

There is one candle that is always lit
            except on Good Friday.
                        This is the sanctuary candle.

This candle is always kept lit as a reminder
that Jesus is present in the tabernacle.
            Really and truly!

Next time you are at Mass
            find the sanctuary candle!
            (It is near the tabernacle.)

Learning about these things
            and thinking about them
                        is an act of love for Jesus.

And we always genuflect respectfully —
            putting our right knee on the floor —
                        whenever we pass the tabernacle.
This is showing our love
            for the presence of our Best Friend,
                        Jesus.

Jesus spoke to them saying,
"I am the light of the world." (John 8:12)

Holy, Holy, Holy

In the language of Jesus' time, there were no words to show
  if something was
    good,
      better,
        or best.
So people would repeat a word
    to show its importance.
For example, the word "Holy"
    means something sacred.

If something was **especially** sacred, it was called "holy, holy."

But a thing that was considered the **most** holy of all
    was called "holy, holy, holy."

At Mass we sing, "Holy, Holy, Holy"
    before the Consecration.
We do this to describe
    the holiest of all things —
      the Eucharist.

Also during Mass,
        we say another prayer three times.
We say:
"Lord, have mercy;
        Christ, have mercy;
                Lord, have mercy."

We do this to ask for Christ's great and wonderful mercy.

Wow!

Learning and understanding
        the important little things we do at Mass
                is a **really big** act of grace.

And our Best Friend, Jesus,
        appreciates that we want to learn about Him.

"Hosanna to the Son of David! Blessed is he who comes in the name of the Lord! Hosanna in the highest!" (Matthew 21:9)

Loving as Jesus Loves

Jesus, our Best Friend, gave us people
        to love us and care for us.
These are our family,
      our friends,
           and even some people
           we don't know yet.
Jesus wants us to be kind to all people.

Most of the time
      it is easy to be kind to people we *like*.
We like to celebrate birthdays
      with family and friends
and we celebrate other special occasions
      with cards and small favors we make
          or save up to buy.
Celebrating family and friends' birthdays
      is a gift to that person
and a "thank-you" to Jesus
      for putting that person in your life.

THE EARTHQUAKE HAS LEFT

32

Jesus wants us to be kind
        even when we are grumpy —
            even when we are upset,
                and even to people
                we don't like.

One way to show kindness for people
        is to pray for them.
When we see a homeless person,
        we can pray for that person.
When there is a terrible hurricane or other disaster
        that leaves people homeless,
                or hurts people,
                        we can do acts of charity.
We can give from our allowance,
        and pray for everyone who was involved!

It especially pleases our Best Friend
        if we are kind to those who are poor
                or need our help.
Being kind to the people Jesus gave us
        is an act of love for Him.

*"Whatever you did for one of these least brothers of
mine, you did for me."* (Matthew 25:45 – NAB)

Holy Smoke!

Ever notice that sometimes at Mass

   the priest
       or the altar server
            swings a pot that makes smoke?

What's happening?
Well, that smoke
     comes from burning something called "incense."
      Using incense this way is a prayer.

Here's how it works!
    The priest puts the incense
        in the pot — called a "censer."
The priest or altar server
    holds the censer in his right hand
and swings the burning incense
    so that the smoke covers the altar,
      or the priest,

        or sometimes
           the Holy Book of
           Scriptures.

Yup — it can be looked at as "holy smoke"
because it's a prayer.

A long time ago, a king named David wrote the Psalms
and sang prayers to God.
He used to say,
"Let my prayers rise to you like incense."
So when the priest incenses something,
it is an offering to God.

Using incense during the Mass
is a wonderful act of grace
and reminds us of the beauty
and mystery
of the Mass.

*Let my prayer be incense before you, my uplifted
hands an evening sacrifice.* (Psalm 141:2 – NAB)

Prayers

It's fun to talk with our friends —
      on the phone,
         at school,
            when we go out to play,
even sometimes when we are supposed to be quiet.

Remember that prayer is talking to God!
He likes to hear us
as we wait for Mass to begin
      and any time we feel sad,
         scared,
            or happy.

He likes it when we tell Him our problems.
He likes to hear us say,
"Thank you, Lord,"
      when something nice happens.
In fact, He even likes it
      when we say short prayers like
"Good morning, Jesus,
      I love you."

Whenever we talk to Jesus, our God —
we can be sure He hears us!

One very special time to pray
    is just before bed.
Our Best Friend loves it when we
    get on our knees
        beside our bed
          and talk to Him.

This is a great time to tell Him about the day
    and thank Him for all of His gifts.
        And tell him our fears or concerns.
It is a wonderful time to say,
"Jesus, I am sorry"
    for anything I may have done
        that hurt you, my Best Friend.

Praying in church, on the way to school,
    or before bed
are all wonderful acts
    of grace toward our Best Friend.

*The fervent prayer of a righteous person is very
powerful.* (James 5:16 – NAB)

Forgiveness

When Jesus died on the cross for us
He did it because He loves us so much
and to forgive us our sins.
What a wonderful gift!

Our friend and Savior wants us
to forgive others, too.

Sometimes forgiving others who
hurt our feelings or exclude us
is really hard to do.
When someone treats us badly,
we sometimes want to stay angry
or feel sorry for ourselves.
Like when someone we thought was a friend
spreads a rumor about us.
Jesus wants us to forgive these people.
This is not an easy thing to do.

But remembering
that Jesus loves
　　　even those who exclude us,
　　　　　as much as He loves us,
may make it easier to forgive.

Recognizing that we
　　　are all God's children
and learning to love others
　　　as He loves us
is a **HUGE** act of grace
　　　that Jesus, our Friend and Savior,
　　　　　loves to see us practice.

"I give you a new commandment, love one another. As I have loved you, so you should also love one another."
(John 13:34 – NAB)

The Gift of Love

There are so many times
      and so many
           big
              and little ways
to share Jesus' friendship
      and to adore Him as Lord.
Each is an act of grace.

Talk to your Best Friend
and give Him the gift of your friendship
      at least once every day.

Imagine each thing you do for Jesus
      as a gift wrapped
          with ribbons of grace
            and a tag marked
"To Jesus with love!"

About the Authors and Illustrator

Rosemarie Gortler is an R.N. and a licensed professional counselor. She is also an extraordinary minister of the Eucharist, a member of the Secular Franciscan Order, and a volunteer for Project Rachel. Rosemarie and her husband, Fred, have five children and nineteen grandchildren.

Donna Piscitelli is a school administrator in Fairfax, Virginia. She is active in her church and in Christian outreach. She and her husband, Stephen, have four children and ten grandchildren.

Mimi Sternhagen is a home-school teacher and mother of five children. She and her husband, Don, assist with Family Life ministry in their parish. In addition to her collaborated works with Rosemarie and Donna, Mimi has illustrated *Catholic Cardlinks: Patron Saints* and *Teach Me About Mary.*

The authors extend their gratitude to Father Richard A. Mullins, administrator of St. Louis Parish in Alexandria, Virginia, for his assistance in the preparation of this book. They also extend a special thank-you to their husbands, Fred Gortler and Steve Piscitelli, for their continued loving support.